Unlocking the Power of Your Amazing Mind

Reduce Stress, Increase Health, Think Positively

Tom Molnar

Unlocking the Power of Your Amazing Mind

Publication Copyright © 2025 by Tom Molnar

ISBN 978-1-7343593-7-4

Apple Valley Press

A big thank you to all those who contributed to make this book possible.

Tom

Why write a book like this? I know that many people, myself included, are often held back by our earliest experiences in life. We often don't know why. In reading through this book, I hope the answers will become clearer. For those of us who are older, we make and often continue to make adjustments. Personally, I was subject to periods of depression, which continued on even during my marriage. My wife would try to encourage me but I usually told her, "Just give me a day or two and it will pass."

As a youth, I tended to be shy and reserved and was never much of a conversationalist until more recent times. I also learned at an early age the bad habit of being critical of everything and everyone—an easy way to lose friends. I saw the glass as half empty instead of half full. It's a sad way to look at the goodness of life. I know now how that came to be for me and it may also be clearer to you later in this book. But I am not alone. Many, if not most of us, have our own personal idiosyncrasies and ways of acting and dealing with life that can be traced back to our earlier experiences. Personally, I am thankful for all the good that has come into my life, including marriage, children and friends.

Unlocking the Power of Your Amazing Mind

Reduce Stress, Increase Health, Think Positively

Our mind controls almost every aspect of our body, including our breathing, heartbeat, temperature, our blood pressure and our immune system to name a few. Most of these internal workings of our body are hidden from our conscious mind. As children, our brains learned automatically the language of our parents, their customs, and the culinary dishes typical of our country.

Ninety five percent of all that we have learned is hidden in our subconscious mind. There, it largely controls our thinking as well as our outlook on life. Even if the conditions during the years we were growing up were not optimal, our brains recorded the difficult times as well as the good times. As children, we were not old enough to process those memories. Now, looking back as adults, we can. Today, we have the power to actually change our outlook on life for the better.

Chapters

Old vs New Learning

When we try to learn something completely new, we have to focus. For example, the first time we are on ice skates we need to focus carefully and follow instructions in order to learn how to do it. Then, once we have learned how to skate, our mind takes over and we don't have to focus carefully anymore. It is the same with riding a bicycle or learning a sport. In tennis, for example, it is a bit complex to throw the ball up in the air and while it's there learn to hit it with our racquet so that it lands in the service area on the opposite court. Once that is mastered, then we can serve with more speed and try to place the ball where our opponent will have the most difficulty hitting it back. That's one of the points of tennis, to win your serve.

Of course, other learning experiences of different kinds are important in all sports. To become proficient in any sport we need to practice. What ordinarily happens when we practice an aspect of a sport over and over again is that the procedure(s) become ingrained in our mind. In time, we don't need to think much about them.

Yes, our mind actually goes into automatic mode. Take, for example, riding a bicycle. The first few times we tried, even with help, it was a bit difficult. Then, once we got the hang of it, riding became easy. That's because our mind has taken over and we don't have to think about how to do it anymore. Once we have learned how to ride and spend some time doing it, the how to do it is kept in our powerful mind. Even if we don't ride again for many years, our unconscious mind remembers, and it is easy for us to mount a bike and take off. We never have to relearn how to ride again.

That is the power of our mind. Once things are learned, our memory retains them. Besides the physical things we learn and our language, the mind is a repository for much more. The memories of our friends and acquaintances, and the experiences we have lived with family and other people is retained. Often not in total, but in general. We may not always remember the name of an old friend we have not seen in a long time, but we remember him or her and the good feelings we have of them when we happen to meet.

Perhaps, unfortunately, we also remember the events and those who have hurt us. We retain lasting memories and sometimes anger at those who have done us wrong. Anger, however, is a two edged sword. The anger we hold in our hearts is actually hurtful to us. It causes us increased stress, anxiety, and can even lead to depression, headaches and other physical symptoms. This can happen even more if one dwells on the anger, relives the events in their mind, and won't let the resentment go. Later, this book will look at practical ways of achieving peace of mind by learning our particular stressors and finding solutions to help in dealing with them.

Our Personal Self Image

Our own personal self image is quite often formed very early in our lives. Similarly, our personalities develop early on. How we perceive ourselves comes from the genes we inherit and to a considerable extent from how we are raised as children. Our experience growing up in our home has so much to do with this. How our parent(s) treated us as babies and young children contributes greatly to our self image and to our personalities. No family raises their child or children in exactly the same way as any other family. In fact, each child within a family has an experience different from any other child living in the same home. Those of us who grew up with a brother, sister or with a number of siblings know that each of us is different. Partly that difference is the result of inheriting different genes from the same parents. Within a family, one child may be outgoing, another thoughtful and another shy. One child may love to be the center of attention, another may prefer alone time with a particular hobby or activity, and another may be very creative while another may be quite pragmatic. Parents who have multiple children are often surprised that each child is so different from the others. Even within the same family, each of us develop our own personality.

Unfortunately, things can go wrong in our early childhood development. Things that can and often do affect us for the rest of our lives. As babies and young children, we need quite a bit of attention and care. We need someone to interact with us, to listen to our early spoken words, and to smile back at us when we develop our first smile.

The importance to us of how we are cared for in our infancy and early years cannot be underestimated. Nevertheless, according to a survey done by the CDC, the majority of Americans have grown up in environments that lacked at least one or many of the qualities that have been determined to be important for our upbringing. Termed Adverse Childhood Experiences, or ACEs, these are potentially traumatic events that occur in childhood, which is listed as between 0 and 17 years of age. In general, those who experienced the least number of adverse experiences during their childhood generally go on to do well in life. However, it has been found that those who experienced a higher number of negative experiences growing up often tend to have greater difficulties even in adult life.

What are these Adverse Childhood Experiences? There are three types: abuse, neglect and household dysfunction. NPR, (National Public Radio) has developed a quiz, called the ACE Quiz that effectively describes the kinds of ACE conditions found to negatively affect children.

1) Before your 18th birthday, did a parent or other adult in the household often or very often...swear at you, insult you, put you down, or humiliate you? *or* act in a way that made you afraid that you might be physically hurt?

2) Before your 18th birthday, did a parent or other adult in the household often or very often...push, grab, slap, or throw something at you? *or* ever hit you so hard that you had marks or were injured?

3) Before your 18th birthday, did an adult or person at least five years older than you ever...touch or fondle you or have you touch their body in a sexual way? *or* attempt or actually have oral, anal or vaginal intercourse with you?

4) Before your eighteenth birthday, did you often or very often feel that...no one in your family loved you or thought you were important or special? *or* your family didn't look out for each other, feel close to each other, or support each other?

5) Before your 18th birthday, did you often or very often feel that...you didn't have enough to eat, had to wear dirty clothes, and had no one to protect you? *or* your parents were too

drunk or high to take care of you or take you to the doctor if you needed it?

6) Before your 18th birthday, was a biological parent ever lost to you through divorce, abandonment, or other reason?

7) Before your 18th birthday, was your mother or stepmother often or very often pushed, grabbed, slapped, or had something thrown at her? *or* sometimes, often, or very often kicked, bitten, hit with a fist, or hit with something hard? *or* ever repeatedly hit over at least a few minutes or threatened with a gun or knife?

8) Before your 18th birthday, did you live with anyone who was a problem drinker or alcoholic, or who used street drugs?

9) Before your 18th birthday, was a household member depressed or mentally ill, or did a household member attempt suicide?

10) Before your 18th birthday, did a household member go to prison?

All these stressful things that can happen in our childhood are not our fault. Sometimes it also may not totally be the fault of parents or caregivers. Alcoholism, for example, can run in families, leaving people with a weakness for it or for other drugs. It is important that the parents of children deal effectively with their substance abuse problems for their unresolved issues will hurt not only themselves but also their children.

A parent who grows up in a family where physical punishment is the rule may continue it with his or her children. However, if done, it must be done with control and in moderation. Loss of a parent through death or divorce is unfortunately relatively common. A parent or caregiver may also experience depression from something that happened in their own life. My mother, for example, lost her mother in a fire when she was only a toddler. No doubt, the experience affected her for the rest of her life. In reality, it affected her children as well.

What is important to realize is that we are not bound by our experiences early in life. We can and do make adjustments. Those who know us best realize our limitations and our idiosyncrasies. For those of us who have suffered any or multiple adverse childhood experiences there is a way to obtain freedom from the past. This will be addressed later in this short book.

The Changed World in Which We Live

For most of us, the world is a much different place than when we were children. Not only are cars faster and computers smaller, but for most of us our personal habits have changed. At the turn of the century, few people had cellphones. Today, most people wouldn't leave home without one. As well, surveys show that, on average, people spend over four hours a day on their phone. Our phone has become a source of information, and for many of us, entertainment. Teens tend to spend even more time than adults. Snapshots of teens today, waiting for an event or for a ride. very often show each of them looking down at their phone.

We live in a communication heavy world. Hours spent watching TV or on our phones can sometimes help us to relax. They can also bring us news from around the world of what is happening. Unfortunately, a big part of the news that is reported deals with crime, tragedies and war. Keeping abreast of what is happening in our town, country and world can be upsetting, especially if watched at length. Shows seldom focus on the good that is done by individuals, schools, churches and charitable institutions. Instead, local news channels and social media sites such as Instagram, Snapchat and even Facebook spend time and money to bring us to unusual and sometimes appalling sites to stimulate our natural desire to learn more. Those who watch a large amount of media news can very easily come to see the world as a dangerous and intimidating place.

The reality is seldom as bad as it may appear. Most of us have friends and relatives, and we can greet our nearby neighbors. The majority of us live in relative comfort in towns, cities and rural areas across America where crime is very infrequent and for the most part unexpected. However, the impression we get from media can be very different. In fact, it can be hard to sleep at night if the news is too distressing. For our own peace of mind, we may need to find ways to relieve ourselves of this stress.

What We Can Do

A simple solution for more contentment is not to watch late news or media outlets that are full of distressing information. Instead, one can read a book, listen to music, pray, meditate or do other things before going to bed. We can take a little time be thankful for all the good things in our life. It is well to focus on them rather than all the troublesome concerns of the world. If time permits, during the day we can take a walk in a park or nature preserve or maybe ride a bicycle. The gradual changes of scenery from Spring to Summer, Fall to Winter can inspire us to take in and appreciate the beauty of nature. If we have a yard, we can plant flowers or even a tree whose beauty we can appreciate all season or all year long.

Many years ago, the differences among people were often attributed to genes. It is true that we all inherit different gene combinations, including children of the same parents. However, there is much more to how we develop and grow than can be described by our genes. The way we were raised is often more likely to influence our personalities than our genes. This will become much more apparent in a later chapter.

While our personal self image tends to continue into adulthood and even old age, our experiences in life can also modify our self perception. Being successful in our work, in our friendships and in marriage, all have positive effects on our how we think of ourselves. The opposite is true as well. Unfortunately, negative employment experiences, broken marriages and inconstant friendships can cause some of us to withdraw. We can blame ourselves or others for problems that come into our lives.

As mentioned, how we were raised in our home can very often have lasting consequences that continue in adulthood and into later life. However, it is important to realize that it is within our power to overcome lasting negative childhood or adult experiences so as to be able to see ourselves and the world in a new light.

We all live with our own personal perceptions of ourselves. Even though we are now older, many of these perceptions we learned as children in the home of our parent(s). If our parents were kind and loving, we are likely to have a good self-image. If not, our personal self-image may be defective. Adding to that, our experiences at school and the treatment we received from our peers also has an important and often lasting effect on our self image. It is quite possible to carry negative feelings about ourselves for the rest of our lives from our experiences at home and at school.

Of course, other circumstances also contribute to our self-image. Our individual successes and failures, our relationships, and today the overwhelming influence of social media, all affect our personal outlook. It can be hard to be at peace with unpaid bills, uncertain employment, and health issues of our own or those of someone we love. It can be hard to be at peace in a chaotic world.

* * *

It is known that our thoughts and attitudes are important not only for our composure but also for our health. Studies show that people who are beset with worries and long term concerns tend to have significantly higher rates of health problems. The state of being anxious is known to be detrimental to heart health and is also linked to a higher incidence of cancer. However, getting a correct diagnosis is important. It is actually true that in some extreme incidences, people who were mistakenly diagnosed with a fatal cancer have died, even though it was later determined that there was no cancer. This shows that what we believe is powerful. It is important that we learn to harness the power of our mind for good, for our own good and for that of others.

The Science Behind the Truth

The important information in this chapter was not always known. In fact, the scientific community in the past believed that our minds were "fixed" and unable to change beyond childhood. Now, however, scientific thinking, based on irrefutable evidence, has in more recent times come to the conclusion that our brains continue to change throughout our lives. The fact that we have the ability to change our mind means that we can develop new skills, new outlooks and also enjoy peace of mind. We can even reduce the likelihood of health problems, including Alzheimer's, as well as change how we think, feel and live our day to day lives.

How does this happen? Within each of our brains are nerve cells, called **neurons** that transmit information and communicate by means of electrical and chemical signals. It has been estimated that there are about 85 billion **neurons** in the brain.

Then, within the space between the neurons are **synapses**. The synapses allow information to pass between the neurons to other neurons so that messages can be communicated to different areas of the brain. Scientists estimate that the total extent of the pathways connecting the neurons or nerve cells in our brain is over 300 miles in length. When we do something repetitively, like making coffee or driving our car, the pathways for these activities are hardwired into our brain so we scarcely need to think about what we are doing. Anytime we repeatedly do something, the pathways begin to form in our minds such that it often becomes automatic for us. Habits, for example, become ingrained within our brains so much so that they can be difficult to break. Curse words after accidentally hitting a finger or thumb with a hammer is an example of an automatic response that comes without thinking for many of us.

What the scientific world is now fully aware of is that new neurons, in a process termed **neurogenesis** are being formed throughout our lives. This means that new thoughts and memories continue to be formed in our brain. Consequently, we are not locked into our past. People of any age have the power to change their brains and their lives for the better.

Despite the fact that we have the power at any time of life to make changes to our brain to change the way we think, it is true that much of our personal ways of thinking are learned early in life. Most psychologists believe that our core personality attributes are formed during our childhood years. However, these can continue to change during adolescence, early adult years, and later in life.

Our relationships with close family members and friends are important in shaping our brains and developing our personalities. Consequently, our thoughts and feelings about family, our self confidence, and even our ability to handle stress tends to be formed in our childhood years. The good news is that we can take steps to transform the fears and personal inadequacies that may have developed when we were children. Authoritative ways and means of doing this will be covered later in this book.

What People and Scripture Say About Changing Our Minds for the Better

"You have the right to change your mind." Oprah Winfrey

"Change your thoughts and you change your world." Norman Vincent Peale

If you can dream it, you can do it." Walt Disney

"You cannot control what happens to you, but you can control your attitude toward what happens to you, and at that, you will be mastering change rather than allowing it to master you." Brian Tracy

"For as he thinks in his heart, so is he." Proverbs 23:7

"Do not be conformed to this world, but be transformed by the renewal of your mind, that by testing you may discern what is the will of God, what is good and acceptable and perfect." Romans 12:2

"Change your thinking, change your life." Ernest Holmes

"The greatest discovery of all time is that a person can change his future by merely changing his attitude."
Oprah Winfrey

"A cheerful heart is good medicine, but a crushed spirit dries up the bones." Proverbs 17:22

"Let all bitterness and wrath and anger and clamor and slander be put away from you, along with all malice; be kind to one another, tenderhearted, forgiving one another, as God in Christ forgave you. ."
Ephesians 4:31-32

"Those who can't change their minds can't change anything." George Bernard Shaw

"Ask, and it will be given to you, seek, and you will find, knock, and it will be opened to you." Matthew 7:7

"Disappointment is temporary. Only your thought about it is permanent. Change your mind about what has disappointed you and you will change your life." Neale Donald Walsch

First Steps in Changing Our Minds

The CDC's assessment is that the majority of people have experienced difficult events in their lives. For this reason, as well as because of the fast pace of modern life, people in general need to find time to relax. We need time to focus and to get back to our own individual life so that we can find contentment. Each of us is different and we all have had different life experiences. For most of us it is helpful and calming to take a step back from the fast pace of our world. This is especially true in the modern era, for today we are bombarded with social media, emails, texts, phone calls, and all manner of interruptions in our personal lives. Our ancestors, even many of our parents, and certainly our grandparents lived their lives almost completely free from these nonstop intrusions into their lives.

It's interesting to take a moment to look back on those "simpler times." Fifty years ago, no one had a personal computer or cellphone. There was no such thing as Facebook or Meta, Snapchat, TikTok, Instagram and a host of other apps. One left home, and if walking, there were no interruptions to your thoughts for no one could call or text you. If in your car, you could turn on your radio but otherwise you kept your eyes on the road as you drove. Unless one was in dense traffic, there was plenty of time for personal reflection even while driving. That's what so many of us miss today, time for reflection. Time to think of our own life as it relates to others.

Today, because of the changed pace of life, we need to set aside some time in our own personal world when we can be free from interruptions. Each of us needs to take time to relax, to relieve stress, and to achieve calmness in our lives. According to the Mayo Clinic, too much stress and tension can lead to heart disease, high blood pressure and diabetes. It can also cause headaches, muscle pain, exhaustion, stomach problems and even depression. There are many easy ways to relieve stress. As to which methods are likely to work best for you, that may depend on your lifestyle and with what you are most comfortable. The following simple practices include many that some of us may already do. They are medically recommended as well.

1) Take a walk or do other exercise: Just a 10-minute brisk stroll can lower anxiety levels. It is known that any kind of exercise boosts mood-regulating chemicals in our brains promoting a better outlook. You might enjoy talking with a friend while walking or exercise but business or other nonsocial calls should be avoided. Walking can be difficult in bitter cold, snow and ice but treadmills that can store vertically are available for a few hundred dollars though an expensive treadmill might cost thousands.

2) Listen to music: Listening to music you like with earbuds, headphones or out loud with speakers helps to drown out cares and put one in a good mood.

3) Deep Breathing: This activates the body's relaxation response. It's easily done. Inhale deeply through your nose allowing your abdomen to expand. Then exhale slowly through your mouth. Take notice of the sensation of your deep breathing and try to relax your muscles each time when you exhale. Once is good, five times is better.

3) Prayer: Short prayers of a few words like "Lord help me," or "Please get me through this," can ease some tension. However, when time permits, a longer period in prayer, either formal or informal, can be more beneficial. This is true especially when one can find a quiet place to pray.

4) Reading: Taking time to read either fiction or nonfiction that is not focused on current events definitely can help to ease one's mind. In this as in prayer, finding a quiet time, perhaps at the end of the day, can really help to rejuvenate one's spirits after a busy or stressful day.

5) Yoga: Yoga is a practice that began in India thousands of years ago. It has become popular worldwide and in recent times in the United States it has ballooned in popularity. Yoga is comprised of three important aspects. Physical, that is obtaining and often holding different bodily positions, meditation, and breathing. Yoga has many physical and mental benefits including improved posture, more flexibility and strength, and body awareness. It can be done alone or in a group. Physically, it can be difficult or relatively simple. One day I opened a door to a small room in our office and was surprised to see one of my fellow workers practicing yoga upside down! Personally, I've participated in "chair yoga," which is far easier.

6) Practice gratitude: It's not surprising that this comes up so frequently as a means to reduce stress. We all have some concerns that if dwelled on too long can become depressing. Yet almost all of us also have some advantage(s) that we can take time to appreciate. One person or family may have a good income, another may have excellent health, another may have an outstanding talent, another may have a wonderfully supportive family, etc. Taking some time to be thankful for our advantages is salutary and can help to minimize stress.

7) Engage in a hobby: Hobbies are far from a waste of time. Whether sitting doing crosswords or other games or actively engaging in sports, workouts or running, any hobby releases feel good chemicals in the body. Whatever you enjoy doing, be it dancing, painting, playing piano or other instrument or any other hobby, know that the pleasure you derive is not only making you happier, it is also making you healthier.

Effects of Personality

The consensus of a large number of psychiatrists as well as many studies indicate that a person's personality is largely formed by the time one is 5 or, in other studies, by 7 years old. This does not mean that one's personality is fully formed at that time, for continued growth in personality can and does continue later in life. What it does mean is that even as children, before we are able to think things through, our personalities become part of who we are. According to psychologists, there are two major factors that influence the development of our personalities. The first is the combination of genes we inherit from our parents and to a certain extent from our grandparents. The other major factor is our early childhood experiences in the homes of our parents or those who raised us.

It is common in college and with some employers to be asked to take personality tests. These tests can help us to learn things about ourselves that may also relate to the world of work. As a quick example, those of us who tend toward being reticent would be unlikely to want or desire to be an actor or actress. So, personality tests are sometimes used to help us and a possible employer decide on our aptitude for a certain kind of job.

One personality inventory that has been around at least since World War II is the Meyer-Briggs personality inventory. Another that has been in use since the 1980's and 1990's is simply called the "Big Five Personality Test" or Five Factor Model. There are, of course, other personality inventories but the Big Five is deemed by many to be the most accurate in describing one's actual personality traits. The test is available online if you should choose to take it.

However, you can get a good idea for yourself of factors in your own personality by looking at the tables below. As you will see, in the Big Five Model, there are five factors, and you can determine for yourself whether you are on the low side or high side or in the middle on each of these five personality traits. Remember, our personalities were formed mostly when we were children, although it is possible later in life to make changes. There is no particular order for these Big Five personality traits but we can start with Extroversion. You may find it interesting and informative to appraise yourself on these factors by marking a place on each line according to the qualities listed below the line.

For example, if you are generally happy you would mark yourself thus on a line between happiness and sadness.

_____ X _____

Or, if you tend toward melancholy, you might mark yourself thus on a line between happiness and sadness.

___ X _____

Of course, if you're in the middle between two traits you can mark it thus:

_____ X _____

Extroversion

High	Low
Outgoing and talkative	Tends to be quiet and reserved
Sociable	Dislikes small talk
Finds it easy to make friends	Likes to have periods of alone time
Likes to start conversations	Doesn't like to be the center of attention
Looks for excitement	Reflective

People who come up high on lists of extroversion include Bill Clinton, Muhammad Ali, Steve Jobs, and Taylor Swift. Those found on low on lists of extroversion include Albert Einstein, Bill Gates, Mark Zuckerberg, and J.K Rowling. Where on the line above would you mark yourself?

Openness

High	Low
Enjoys learning/trying new things	Dislikes change
Likes to travel	Prefers to avoid taking risks
Enjoys challenges	Holds to traditional thinking
Has a wide range of interests	Likes to stick to routines
Has an active imagination	Is more grounded

People who tend to be ranked high in openness include Jeff Bezos, Larry Page, Oprah Winfrey and Nelson Mandela. While it may be difficult to find famous people known for their lack of openness, many people from all walks of life who work in factories, sales, banking, real estate, and education, etc. can be low on openness. Where on the above line would you mark yourself?

Agreeableness

High	**Low**
Even tempered	Competitive
Kind to others	Less likely to help others
Compassionate	Uncooperative
Helpful and generous	Antagonistic
Trustworthy	Selfish

Some well known people who are noted for being agreeable are Mother Teresa, Steve Carell, Keanu Reeves and Ryan Reynolds. Those who some consider to have more disagreeable traits include Kanye West, Mariah Carey, Charlie Sheen and Kathy Griffin. Where would you mark yourself on the line?

Conscientiousness

High	Low
Dependable	Often acts on impulse
Well organized	Not especially neat and tidy
Self-disciplined	Jumps from one thing to another
Good at planning	Is prone to be late
Mindful of deadlines	Not always dependable

A few people who are known to be conscientious include music director John Williams, famed soccer player David Beckham, Oprah Winfrey and Fred (Mister) Rodgers. Notable non conscientious people are harder to find, likely because it takes effort to succeed in almost any field. However, some artists may make it with innate talent as well as some musicians. On the negative side, highly conscientious people are generally successful but may find it difficult to take time off to relax and enjoy the moment. Those low on the conscientiousness scale are typically always ready to enjoy a good time.

Neuroticism +

High	Low
Often feels insecure	Tends to be optimistic
Gets stressed easily	Able to manage stress
Tends to worry a lot	Tends to be confident
Sensitive and easily upset	Often feels relaxed
Experiences mood swings	Emotionally stable

A sizeable percentage of the population deals with neuroticism or emotional instability. Many famous people, including Albert Einstein and Winston Churchill dealt with negative feelings. Well known people of today who speak of their difficult emotions include actress Keira Knightly, singer, Adele, Prince Harry, Kevin Love, of basketball fame, and singers Selena Gomez and Lady Gaga. Dealing with emotional instability makes life more difficult and can lead to drug and alcohol problems. Today, however, more than ever in the past, medication is helping people to relieve stress. Where would you mark yourself on the line above

We are all different. Which of the above traits is high for you, low, or in between?

Some Words About Personality Inventories

The proceeding run through of the Big Five Model can give us some ideas about ourselves as well as about other people. However, it should not be taken as definitive. Taking the Big Five test itself or the also popular Briggs Meyer personality inventory may give some refinement to the picture of ourself that results from marking our position on the above lines. However, our personalities are not written in stone. If we happen to be feeling down in the dumps when taking the inventory, our results and thoughts of ourselves may be significantly different than if we are feeling hale and hearty.

Nevertheless, looking at where we marked ourselves on the lines above can give us some additional knowledge about ourselves and also about others. As human beings, almost all of us have quite different personalities. One person may love to be in the limelight, or to be the life of the party, and another would feel very uneasy to be on stage or to have any kind of spotlight focused on them. Similarly, many people are very conscientious to take all the steps necessary to achieve some success in life endeavors while others are happier to take life as it comes and enjoy the moment. They're less concerned with deadlines and arriving "on time."

It helps to recognize that many people are often very different than us. Not long ago I was shocked to see a child throw from a car what looked like a complete dinner package with wrappers, cups and paper onto a street in our neighborhood. I was driving behind their car and continued on my way and saw that the car stopped at a nearby doctor's office. I didn't pause to say anything to them, but thinking about it later I realize that the child had likely had no training in conscientiousness. We adults know that it is against the law to litter, although I'm sure some of the trash on the highway comes from people who care less.

So, to get back to the point, we may have found that we are high in some aspects of the Big Five inventory and low in others. Each one of us is different and we fit into our family and our society in different ways. We may have strengths in one or more areas while others have strengths in other areas. Of course, these aspects of personality can and often do change over time. A person may start off rather shy and reticent and end up later in life being quite comfortable in engaging in social conversations with people who have different viewpoints.

In the same way a person who worries a lot and who deals with mood swings may in time learn to be more comfortable and relaxed. In general, it has been determined that as people grow older, they tend to be not quite as open to new ideas and somewhat more resistant to change. It's understandable. They've lived their lives in a certain way, their own way, why change in one's senior years?

The Big Five and the World of Work

As mentioned, many colleges and some employers use the Big Five personality inventory. This can help students know more about themselves and employers know if a job applicant is a good fit.

The world of work is huge, with so many varieties and types of jobs and specialties not available many years ago. And, of course, many career paths require extensive education and training. A short book like this cannot begin to be comprehensive enough to list all the possibilities. However, it can help to give some direction toward careers in line with personality inventories.

For those of us who are older, career paths no longer matter for us though for our children and grandchildren they are important. There are few things worse than to pay expensive tuition for training that one doesn't use or to be stuck in a job that you hate.

The following then are general guidelines that give a sampling of career choices based on personality. They are certainly not hard and fast guides, for there are always exceptions. However, they should be instructive in general for those who are preparing to enter or change employment. To be more certain of your personality type, if using it to help in a career choice, it might be helpful to take one of the free online inventories. Most of them take only thirty minutes or so to complete.

Some Jobs for Those High in Extroversion

Sales jobs of all kinds.
Marketing managers
Service and hospitality—includes waiters/waitresses, bartenders, hotel staff, etc.
Public relations specialists.
Actors and actresses

All these jobs and many more feature considerable continuous contact with people.

Employment, Those High in Agreeableness

Nursing and health care specialties
Speech therapists
Counselors
Teachers
Child care workers
Social workers

All these, and related jobs, depend on one-on-one **supportive** contact with people.

Jobs for Conscientious People

Accountant
Project manager
Engineers
Data Analysts
Construction workers, electricians, plumbers, carpenters, ironworkers, etc.
Doctors/dentists

These kinds of jobs require very much attention to detail and thus work well for those high in conscientiousness.

For Those High in Neuroticism

Freelance work—flexibility, can set own schedule.
Art, Writing, Music—provides outlets for creative expression.
Graphic design
Mental Health Counselor—understanding others who have emotional challenges.
Animal caretaker—for those who love animals
Librarian

These careers often offer flexibility and engagement for those who score high in anxiety.

Some Careers for Those High in Openness

Artist
Writer—authors and poets
Software developer
Research scientist
Airplane pilot

These types of jobs are often right for people who enjoy developing new ideas and exploring imaginative concepts. Such persons are usually bored with doing repetitive tasks.

Stress Matters

According to the CDC and a host of other sources, most of us have lived through at least one Adverse Childhood Experience. Many others of us have also dealt with major life experiences that may well have left a permanent mark on our psyche. Things like the death of a family member, divorce, loss of employment, a major injury or disease and a host of other traumatic things can affect us for a very long time. In fact, we may still be living with or reliving these major events. It takes time to heal both in our bodies and in our minds.

We have a clear awareness of when our body is healed after injury or sickness. If we do have a full recovery from an injury, we can take steps to gradually return to our former physical condition. Either that, or we will have to work around any bodily limitations.

Unfortunately, we have no such clear awareness of how our subconscious mind has recorded and remembers the major events in our lives. Our minds retain the hurt and the pain we may have felt both as a result of injuries and also as a result of difficult times in our life going all the way back to our early childhood. We may not be able to consciously recall any times as children when we were mistreated, when we were harmed or when we were unloved. Nevertheless, the feelings left from these kinds of events are faithfully recorded in our subconscious. This thinking can make us feel that we are unworthy, that we are unlovable and even that we can never be successful in life. They can also be a source of worry, of hypersensitivity and also of dissatisfaction with life. They can effectively make it difficult for one to live in the present moment and enjoy life.

Fortunately, not everyone is affected by negative subconscious programing. However, many people are, and most of us can benefit from alleviating much of the stress in our lives. The next chapter will take a look at how unresolved stress can have an effect on our lives.

Signs of Unresolved Distress

The following are some relatively common signs that one may be dealing with unresolved issues affecting thinking. There are many helping agencies that address these concerns. The list below comes from Cornerstone Healing Center in Scottsdale, Arizona and The Integrative Life Center in Nashville, Tennessee. The concerns they address are quite similar. I have listed them numerically but in reality, they have no particular order.

1) **Low Self-Esteem:** Feelings of inadequacy or unworthiness may stem from lacking acceptance, usually early in life. Often, a critical inner voice makes one's person or efforts seem substandard.

2) **Avoidance or Strong Reactions:** Avoiding certain people or places or experiencing fear or

discomfort when near them may result if the person or place caused you trauma in the past.

3) **Trust Issues:** Not trusting others or a fear of expressing your true feelings to another can result if previous experiences made you feel vulnerable or unsafe.

4) **Attachment Issues:** Difficulty making close friends either because of avoidance, or becoming excessively dependent can result from unmet needs. It can occur even when one in a secure relationship. This happens when a person feels anxious when their partner plans to leave for an outing or take an out of town trip without you.

5) **Difficulty Regulating Emotions:** Quickly going from calm to upset or even fearful over the everyday actions of others or by some small change you notice that quickly arouses your emotions in a surprising way. This can result from something negative that is stuck in your memory from long ago.

6) **Dissociative Experiences:** Feeling disconnected from yourself or from those around you for a shorter or longer period of time is a way to deal with severe stress. If aroused by something in your past it can become recurrent and indicate those feelings need to be resolved.

7) **Anxiety or Hypervigilance:** Persistent anxiety or the feeling of needing to be on your guard even in safe places is usually the result of past trauma. Calming exercises can be beneficial.

8) **Difficulty Coping with Change:** Life has many ups and downs aside from major events. Throwing

a temper tantrum as an adult when things don't go your way or lashing out at others in a more or less childlike manner is indicative of an unresolved early trauma.

9) **Memory Loss:** Sometimes we don't remember things as they really were, especially if the event was traumatic. In one way, this can protect us from dwelling on an extremely difficult event or series of events. However, to completely recover, it is important to be able to see what actually did happen.

Going Forward

Many of us do not necessarily experience the unresolved stress signals mentioned in the previous section. Still, every one of us has concerns and issues that are part of living in a complex world. A world that, through media, brings us upsetting things and events happening in our nation and around the world. Unfortunately, tuning out is not easy for we are bombarded with information from so many sources.

Besides news, we are also bombarded with seemingly nonstop advertising. No matter where we look, things are being advertised. Of course, the constant ads also have their effect on us.

For many years now we see it even on our email accounts and almost from the beginning of television it was there. The United States allows more advertising minutes on TV shows than most nations do, such that in an hour of programming there may be twenty or more minutes of ads. When watching sporting events, one often hears and sees advertising messages even while the game is ongoing.

What are the ads for? Obviously for us to spend money and buy the products. The ad companies are smart, many are multimillion dollar companies, who bring together the best people and visuals to influence our buying decisions. They know what is psychologically motivating for people. We are encouraged through advertising to buy more, often much more than we actually need. We can even feel a sense of unhappiness because we don't have all the wonderful things that appear in advertisements.

You may notice that rarely are inexpensive cars advertised on television. Instead, an abundance of powerful pickup trucks and sleek, generally expensive sedans are presented. One vehicle that has long been popular is the Jeep in all its various models. This, you may have learned, was the vehicle that "won the war," that is World War II. However, the present Jeep Wrangler, while retaining the same basic shape, is far larger and heavier. It is a robust design and is offroad capable but unfortunately, according to Consumers Reports and other sources, it is one of less reliable cars on the road. Too bad, I really like the look.

Another product that seems to be continuously advertised is medicine. However, we are extremely unlikely to see aspirin, Tylenol or antacids appear in television ads. No, those that are advertised are medications requiring prescriptions. Sometimes I curiously look up the cost of the medicine being advertised. Surprisingly, at least to me, most of them cost thousands of dollars a month, unless you have quite good insurance. Because of regulations, these ads also quickly list a host of negative effects that may result from taking the medications, including death. Nevertheless, the people shown in the ads seem to be enjoying life, interacting with their children and grandchildren, having a good time despite their various debilitating conditions. Of course, the implication is that their new delight in life is possible because of the medicine they are taking.

Obviously, the ads are effective because even though ad time is expensive, they would not be continued unless they were profitable. The advertisements often do have the effect of making many people want what they are portraying. Is it all good? Maybe, in some cases. Personally, as for cars, I would rather have wonderful vacations than expensive vehicles. Many of us do have choices.

Speaking of handling money, one of the most deleterious practices is to buy something using a credit card and then not immediately pay off the monthly balance. The interest rates on credit cards are monstrous—typically adding monthly charges of between 18% and 29%. Delay in paying off credit card debt can more than double the cost of items purchased. For many things, with likely exceptions for big items, like a house, auto or replacing a furnace or air conditioner, it is financially beneficial to wait until they can be purchased outright. However, there are many options these days, even for Amazon purchases, of paying a part of the cost at once and the rest later.

One financial adviser recommends waiting a day before making a partial payment on an item. That way one can tell if it's really essential or not. Of course, for large expenditures, getting a bank loan is far cheaper than using a credit card.

There is a way to evade the continuous ads that come when watching television. I learned it from my brother-in-law and it's easy. With remote in hand, simply mute the commercial time. Having a book or magazine to look at during lengthy commercials is also helpful. As well, some shows and films will let you skip through the ads, that is if you start watching twenty minutes or so after the show has started. It works even for many televised sporting events.

Toward Peace of Mind

Despite living in a world saturated with advertising and focused on war and crime, there are ways to calm our hearts and minds and find composure. This is true, even for those who have suffered trauma in their lives. Some of the ways to achieve this have been in use since ancient times and others are much more modern. Although life is more complex today, it is unlikely that human beings as people have changed at all in thousands of years.

Affirmation

Affirmation is an important way of overcoming negative thoughts about yourself, especially those that may have occurred in childhood years. It is very easy to do and it is important that it be done repeatedly. The best times to do it are just when you are going to sleep at night and the first thing upon arising in the morning. It is helpful to repeat your affirmation during the day as well.

What you say to yourself in words of affirmation are important and are related to your personal situation. For anyone who has felt spurned or put down early in life a good one is **"I am a loving person deserving of love."** Another could be "I **am good, people see that in me."** It is best, as in these examples, not to use the word **will** because it is not as powerful as the word **am.**

It must be stated that it is very important that one continues this each day, preferably twice a day to get results. What you are doing is planting in your subconscious mind that you are a worthy person, thus overcoming anything to the contrary. But it must be done repeatedly to be effective. Dr. Caroline Leaf, a cognitive neuroscientist recommends to do it for a minimum of 21 days. Others say "three to four weeks" and some say considerably longer. Then, what is likely to happen over the course of weeks and months of repeating your affirmation is that you actually change for the better. (Not that you were bad to begin with.) That's because you and your subconscious mind will begin to see yourself as a worthy person, both able to receive love and able to give love. You may find that relatively small things, such as opening a door for someone, letting a car into your lane, or greeting people may become more natural for you. You will feel better about yourself, find it easier to be more sociable around people, and may even begin to make new lasting friendships. That's the power of consistently repeating to yourself your words of affirmation.

Mindfulness

Mindfulness helps one to deal with negative thoughts or influences. It is a quick way to achieve a feeling of calmness in one's life. It is quite easy to do, requiring only a few minutes to master. One needs a quiet time, when all distractions are turned off. It can be done in a relatively short time, minutes, or can extend for a half hour or longer.

It is helpful to assume a relaxed position and to pay attention to your breathing. It is often recommended to breathe in relatively slowly through your nose and then exhale slowly through your lips. The idea is to fully engage yourself in the moment, taking note of your breathing and freeing yourself from thoughts of the past or the future.

Observe your own body quietly and remain in the present moment. Your mind may wander to the future or to the past but gently bring it back to the calm, peaceful present. You may experience quiet sounds like the refrigerator or furnace running or hear the chirping of birds, etc. The experience of mindfulness helps to return your mind to a calm, comfortable state. Acceptance of your present state is key.

The intention of mindfulness is to become comfortable in your own body. In the unlikely event that a past emotional trauma rises up that is too much, stop immediately and do something, anything to take your mind off the event until you are in a more relaxed state. In general, mindfulness is very helpful overall in reducing stress, anxiety and negative emotions. Mindfulness can be experienced daily at a certain time or at any time of the day. As with the practice of affirmation, it is helpful to get into a routine where mindfulness becomes easy and natural for you.

Journaling—Taking Note

A highly recommended activity, journaling involves keeping a notebook where you can write down (or type) your thoughts and feelings. They can be written briefly, one sentence to a few, or can go on for much longer. A good way to start is to simply start with a blank page and write whatever comes to mind. Then, things may come out from the past or the present that may be more difficult to process. What writing does is to objectify them, putting them there in front of you.

At first, it may be a bit harder to focus on the exact nature of what happened, or your personal feelings about the events or incidents. However, with practice it becomes easier to do. By writing them down, it is easier to see the concerns for what they are. Thinking about times or incidents that happened in the past is helpful, especially when we can look back and view them in the present. This makes old problems and

55

concerns simpler to visualize and to handle. Especially looking at situations that may have been hurtful to us as children, seeing them with an adult mind can put them in perspective and can enable us to move forward in the present.

It may happen that as one looks at what has been written, strong emotions may arise. If they are troubling, it is usually best to stop at that point and take a breather. Doing things like taking a walk, listening to music, deep breathing, or talking with a friend can help.

The point of journaling is to help with our processing of events and emotions that can and often do have a lasting influence in our lives. By seeing them objectively and taking time to think about past events the goal is to see them better in the light of day, as a thinking adult, so as to resolve them in our mind. Daily journaling, whether short or long, can help to put things in perspective. If not daily, even once or twice a week can be beneficial. Then, having done it for a while, looking over your past notes is often very helpful in seeing progress in dealing with areas of concern.

Talking Things Out

Especially helpful in resolving stress is talking things out. Finding someone you trust who is a good listener is important. Oftentimes, people tend to be too quick to give their opinions, interrupting what you need to say to get the whole story out. Ask them to listen before commenting. It's not always easy to confide your deep thoughts to others but if you can find someone you can trust, talking with them can help one to see problems and concerns in a better light. Such "talk therapy" with a friend or relative can be of immense benefit in shedding new light on concerns and can be very helpful in relieving stress. Of course, professional therapists are also usually available and they are trained to deal with people problems for a fee. It is not always necessary to schedule a visit. Today it is far easier and often less expensive to connect with a therapist by phone or through a medium such as zoom. However, evaluate the helpfulness of a particular caregiver. Most, but not all, give good advice.

Heartbreak

Heartbreak happens a lot. It usually accompanies the death of a spouse, certainly at the death of a child, and usually when marriages or close relationships end. Unfortunately, death is the lot of human beings, a fact that doesn't make it any easier to handle.

What can be done if one loses the love of his or her life, or if a parent or someone else close to us is now gone from us forever? Each person's reaction to loss can be different. There will be a period of mourning that may be expressed in different ways. There is very often a desire to withdraw to help us process in our minds the full impact of the loss of a loved one.

However, one can withdraw too far, such that others who would like to console us may be turned away. If the time of deep mourning goes on too long it can turn into depression. Eventually, it is necessary, despite our loss, to return to the world of work or study that is our own typical way of being in the world. It is important, despite our low spirits, to rejoin the world and engage with family and friends in meaningful ways. Especially after a major loss it does one no good to become a loner. We are human beings and as such we need social interaction.

I could speak of my own losses. One that was devastating for me was when my fiancée unexpectedly terminated our engagement at the worst time, days after I lost my job. Another was when I came home to see my father lying on the floor dead of a heart attack at the relatively young age of 59.

We all have losses and they are definitely not easy to accept. Yet, in time we have to move on. We need to reengage with the world and make the best of our lives going forward. We need to be with people, to be with friends and relatives. For most of us with religious belief, certainly Christians, Muslims and Jews, a happy afterlife awaits us where we will enjoy being in the presence of God and the saints. Then, we can look forward to reuniting in joy with all those loved ones who have gone before us.

Thinking Positively

Selected Words of Wisdom

These selections come from many different sources, from men, women, historical people, from celebrities, a few from the Bible and others that are just for fun. Read a few at a time or many. You might check off or underline any you want to remember. Enjoy!

"Once you replace negative thoughts with positive ones, you'll start having positive results." —Willie Nelson

"The mind is everything. What you think you become." – Buddha

"The way I see it, if you want the rainbow, you gotta put up with the rain." – Dolly Parton

"A day without sunshine is like, you know, night."—Steve Martin

"Just one small positive thought in the morning can change your whole day."
– Dalai Lama

"Believe you can and you're halfway there."
– Theodore Roosevelt

Don't compare yourself to others. You are unique, and you have your own path to follow. Focus on your own journey, and celebrate your own successes. –Unknown

"Where there's hope, there's life. It fills us with fresh courage and makes us strong again." — Anne Frank

"Peace I leave with you; my peace I give you. I do not give to you as the world gives. Do not let your hearts be troubled and do not be afraid." — John 14:27

Stay positive and maintain a grateful heart. A positive mindset can work wonders, and gratitude can transform your perspective on life. Unknown

"Try to be a rainbow in someone else's cloud." —*Maya Angelou*

"Success comes in cans; failure in cant's."– Unknown

You are stronger than you think, and you have the ability to overcome any obstacle. Don't let fear hold you back. Embrace challenges as opportunities to grow and learn. –Unknown

"If I'd have done all the things I was supposed to have done, I'd be really tired."– Willie Nelson

"I love being married. It's so great to find one special person you want to annoy for the rest of your life." — Rita Rudner

Never give up on yourself. You are worth the effort, and you deserve to live a life you love. Keep pushing forward, no matter what. –Unknown

"Happiness is not something readymade; it comes from your own actions." —The Dalai Lama

"The miracle is not that we do this work, but that we are happy to do it." —Mother Theresa

"If you want to lift yourself up, lift up someone else." —Booker T. Washington

Mark 11:24: Therefore I tell you, whatever you ask in prayer, believe that you have received it, and it will be yours.

"A diamond is merely a lump of coal that did well under pressure." –Unknown

"Before you criticize someone, you should walk a mile in their shoes. That way when you criticize them, you are a mile away from them and you have their shoes." – Jack Handey

"Accept who you are. Unless you're a serial killer." — Ellen DeGeneres

"Always forgive your enemies; nothing annoys them so much." — Oscar Wilde

"Love is blind but marriage is a real eye-opener." — Pauline Thomason

"True friends are those who really know you but love you anyway." — Edna Buchanan

"The secret of staying young is to live honestly, eat slowly, and lie about your age." — Lucille Ball

"Smile in the mirror. Do that every morning and you'll start to see a big difference in your life."– Yoko Ono

"No act of kindness, no matter how small, is ever wasted."– Aesop

"I'd like to live like a poor man – only with lots of money."– Pablo Picasso

"Anxiety weighs down the heart, but a kind word cheers it up." – Proverbs 12:25

"The greater part of our happiness or misery depends upon our dispositions, and not upon our circumstances."– Martha Washington

"Life is 10 percent what happens to me and 90 percent how I react to it" – Charles Swindoll

"For every failure, there's an alternative course of action. You just have to find it. When you come to a road block, take a detour." Mary Kay Ash

"Our prime purpose in this life is to help others. And if you can't help them, at least don't hurt them."– Dalai Lama

"Your vocation in life is where your greatest joy meets the world's greatest need."
– Frederick Buechner

"No matter what happens in life, be good to people. Being good to people is a wonderful legacy to leave behind."– Taylor Swift

If you do not change direction, you might end up where you are heading. Lao Tzu

Be yourself. Everyone else is already taken. -- Oscar Wilde

"If you have made mistakes, there is always another chance for you. You may have a fresh start any moment you choose, for this thing we call 'failure' is not the falling down, but the staying down." Mary Pickford

"No one can make you feel inferior without your consent." Eleanor Roosevelt

"It's not whether you get knocked down, it's whether you get up." Vince Lombardi

Come to me, all who labor and are heavy laden, and I will give you rest. Matthew 11:28:

"You are never too old to set another goal or to dream a new dream." C. S. Lewis

"The secret of getting ahead is getting started." – Mark Twain

"Do not be anxious about anything, but in every situation, by prayer and petition, with thanksgiving, present your requests to God. And the peace of God, which transcends all understanding, will guard your hearts and your minds in Christ Jesus." – Philippians 4:6-7

"Take care of your body. It's the only place you have to live." – Jim Rohn

"Change your thoughts and you change your world." – Norman Vincent Peale

"Never let the odds keep you from doing what you know in your heart you were meant to do." H. Jackson Brown, Jr.

"Anyone who stops learning is old, whether twenty or eighty. Anyone who keeps learning stays young. The greatest thing you can do is keep your mind young." – Mark Twain

"Our greatest glory is not in never falling, but in rising every time we fall." — Confucius

Remember that not getting what you want is sometimes a wonderful stroke of luck. Dali Lama

"Since you get more joy out of giving joy to others, you should put a good deal of thought into the happiness that you are able to give"—Eleanor Roosevelt

"Don't let the hard days win." Seen on a shirt a man was wearing.

If you liked this book, consider giving a short review of it on the book's Amazon page. It's appreciated. Reviews help a book to be seen by others who may be interested in similar works.

If you've never done it before it is easy and confidential. (I believe Amazon may have a policy that one must have spent $50 on their site in the past year to post a review.)

To do a review, simply scroll down when on the book page and look to the left side where there may be other reviews and click on the space below "Review this product." It will ask the number of stars you give it, five or four is good and then you can make a short or longer statement relating to the book. Thank you!

Some of Tom's Other Books

Time Out for Happiness

Not everyone grows up in a happy home with loving parents. I didn't. Today, most of us don't experience enough happiness in our daily lives. Anyone can feel downhearted. The key is knowing the ways to overcome our sadness.

Increasing happiness is much easier if we know how. Unfortunately, many of the ways commonly thought to bring happiness are wrong. This is proven by observation as well as by scientific studies.

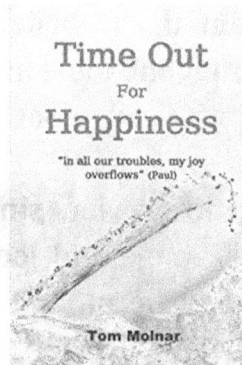

Time Out
For
Happiness

"in all our troubles, my joy overflows" (Paul)

Tom Molnar

Time Out for Happiness delivers insightful thinking on how to minimize sadness and increase joy. It features quick pick me ups as well as longer term strategies. Once we discard the ways that don't bring happiness and focus on those that do, like sharing with others, we will be well on our way to living a happier life. The truths found in this book are affirmed by those who have spent much of their working lives finding real answers to what brings happiness and joy.

Swept Away

Swept Away draws from Civil War records, from accounts of life in the times, and from a true love story. It brings to life the story of Jenny, a girl turning 18 as the war begins. It finds her caught up in the love of a man for whom she is only his "best friend."

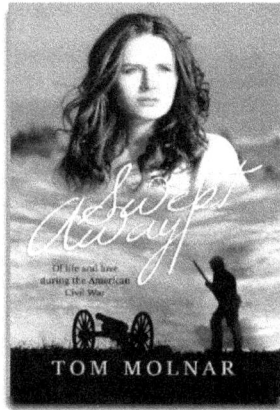

When Daniel leaves to fight for the South, Jenny's small town and her father's farm are soon occupied by hated Yankee soldiers. One of them, a Union captain, has the audacity to smile at her.

As the war intensifies, Jenny will find courage to do things she never thought she would do, and she will see things she never thought she would see.

Swept Away brings home the reality of war as well as life as it was lived in rural America. It is Jenny's story, one of love, the unexpected, and beginning anew.

Wired for Love

We all need love, from the strongest man to the most delicate woman. Young children, without love, are likely to die. All evidence shows that we human beings are genetically "hard wired" to give and receive love. In its absence, studies show that we tend to die sooner and experience far less happiness in our lives.

Our "attachment style," affects how we love and whom we love, and even those with whom we find it easiest to get along. Now, we are able to learn our own attachment style and that of our partner. The bonus is that in doing so we are likely build our esteem and increase our happiness as well as the happiness of the one we love.

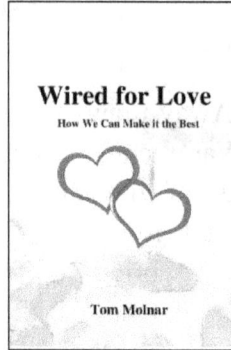

Wired for Love
How We Can Make it the Best

Tom Molnar

All titles are available on Amazon

Dark Age Maiden

Dark Age Maiden is an adventurous tale—with a bit of romance. It tells the dramatic story of how Europeans turned back the Muslim advance that had already conquered Africa and Spain. The famous Battle of Tours in 732 AD saved Europe from Muslim domination and changed history. A fictional account based on real events and

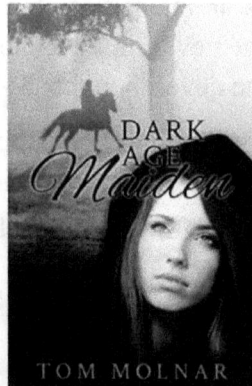

DARK AGE Maiden

TOM MOLNAR

Recent Nonfiction

Jesus, Kind, Loving, Dangerous

The Pharisees realized right away that Jesus was a dangerous man. He was breaking their religious laws and keeping company with sinners. Ultimately, they had him crucified.

JESUS
KIND, LOVING,
DANGEROUS
Tom Molnar

We, however, often get the watered down version of Jesus depicted in books and movies. He doesn't seem dangerous to us, but he is. His life changing message is not one of following laws, but of transforming hearts.

The Universe of God and Humanity

Start with Adam and Eve and add evolution—two different stories or do they come together? Then add the discoveries that even Einstein couldn't believe, ones that have now quietly become a fact of life. Discoveries that have the power to change our view of God and the universe.

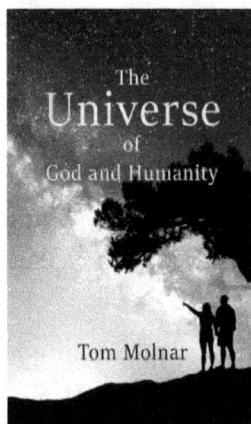

Already, the unexpected power of quantum mechanics is being used in our everyday lives, in cell phones, in lasers and at store checkout counters. What are the strange qualities of matter that can change how we look not only at the universe but also God and creation?

Mary, the Girl Who Said Yes

Mary's story is one of danger and excitement, love, sorrow and uncertainty. She had to be strong to face the trials that would come. Delving into her life as seen in the Gospels shows a spirited and courageous woman, a fitting mother for Jesus, the man of God who changed history.

"A good overview of Mary and the times she lived in. Very nicely done." Rev. Joseph Hannon S.D.B., St. Petersburg, Florida.

"I very much enjoyed your reflections on Mary," Bishop Dale Melczek.

An interesting story told in a clever manner." Suzy Watts, book reviewer.